MY BIG BROTHER

By: Gloria Abioye
Illustrated :Ambadi Kumar

First Edition

Copyright © Gloria Abioye

All rights reserved.
Published by The Lighthouse books, Agape Inc.

No part of this book may be reproduced, stored in a retrieval system, or transmitted in any form or by any means, electronic, mechanical photocopying, recording, or otherwise without written permission of the publisher.

For information regarding permission, write to:
thelighthousemain@gmail.com

ISBN: 978-1-950320-14-1
Visit us at:
www.thelighthousebooks.com
Printed in the USA

Introduction

Dear Parents,

Most children like to hang out with each other in the home and the older ones play very important roles in being good role models to the younger ones.

The younger tends to do or follow in the footstep of the older and it is imperative that a culture of respect, dignity, love and togetherness is developed among siblings.

This real-life narrative of a young boy and the pictures he sees in a brother and family are put into words. The roles of a big brother are vital in a family and it is important that all siblings and parents are involved in a lifelong growth and togetherness of the family.

My family, my everything!

This account of the young boy will give your family ideas of what boys (girls included) can do for fun, keep busy, the goodness shared by siblings and parents' involvement in this healthy relationship.

Gloria A Abioye
Mother & Author

My name is Shalum, but my friends call me Shasha.

I am eleven years old and I live in a single-family home in a quiet neighborhood. I love to play, read and make new friends and something I do for fun is playing Basketball with my brothers.

When we start to play basketball, my neighborhood friends also join us, and playing becomes so much more interesting and fun.

I have two brothers, one older and one younger.

My big brother loves me and always teases me in order for me to smile and laugh. He helps with my homework and house chores and I always look to him when I need help.

When things get broken around the house, he is the expert who fixes things.

My big brother is strong, energetic, intelligent, smart and very considerate; I love to hang out with him a lot.

My brother is tall, 11 inches taller than me. He is 5 feet, 5 inches. Little brother, who is 7 years old, wanted to know how height is measured. I told him that one foot is 12 inches

My brothers and I enjoy playing musical instruments, and so our parents have private instructors for us who coach us in playing the keyboard, which is also called the piano.

We practice and play to all kinds of music, and we love to show our skills during talent shows in my local church. I also play the keyboard while the choir sings in our church services.

My big brother loves to draw pictures and images. He likes manga art, superheroes and anime, which are cartoons from Japan.

One of our favorite places to go to is the Public Library. At the library we have lots of books and magazines to check out and bring home for our reading. We do check out DVD's when we need to and we also enjoy the access we have to the computers to play and learn from.

The library is very educational and a great learning place for every kid.

Big brother looked forward to being a teenager and when his birthday finally came ,it was a celebration time. I now esteem him so much and wish I could also become a teenager immediately. Parents advised that being a teenager comes with so much responsibility and carefulness. A teenager learns to care for his or her body, room, the home, younger ones and would have to read more. In fact he can now babysit a baby if he wants.

Because he is 13 years old now, mom has started teaching big brother to cook.

He makes pancakes, waffles, and eggs for our breakfast. He can boil rice, chicken and vegetables. He always bakes our pizza, chicken, chicken nuggets and chicken wings. He likes to eat these foods and a lot of cookies.

Mom says eating cookies, donuts, ice cream and other sweets is not healthy for the body and our teeth.

Today, my brothers and I went for a physical checkup and examination of our body in the clinic. The pediatrician examined us closely and encouraged us to eat more of vegetables, fruit and milk and of course to take less sugary food. Mom helps with the food preparation making sure we have more healthy choices on our plates.

After the Clinic visit, we started doing some exercises and physical training at our home and in the neighborhood recreation center.

At the recreation center, we have various activities to choose from, we can swim, make art works, engage in seasonal league competition of soccer, volleyball, basketball, flag football, wrestling, and many more other sports and games.

Big brother does a lot of exercises at home which I secretly admire him for. Me and my brothers run, do jumping jacks, do some jump ropes and in fact, follow a trainer app on our tablet.

It's always fun when my dad leads, and my mom joins us in these physical training and exercises. It encourages us and make us want to do more.

It's sometimes hard to part with each other at night before we go to bed. My brother lets me sleep in his room when I want to, and especially during the weekends. I think having a big brother who is strong, big and bold is the best that one can have.

Shortly before we go to bed, Dad, Mom, my brothers, and I exchange hugs and kisses with each other, and we pray for each other to a sweet dream and beautiful morning to come.

My Big Brother is:

B - Bold
I - Intelligent
G - Gifted

B - Brave
R - Robust
O - Outstanding
T - Thoughtful
H - Helpful
E - Exceptional
R - Rugged

About the Author

Gloria Abioye is a wife and mother who currently works as an IT Security Specialist. The yearn to read and write books started as a young girl from the school library where her father was a school Principal. With an unlimited access to books, she developed a passion to read every available book, encyclopedia and daily newspaper present in the small library. She proceeded to write stories and publications in the children's corner of her State newspaper – "The Herald" as at the time.

A mother of three children, all boys and happily married to her understanding and supportive husband – Femi for 15 years. She likes solving word puzzles, cooking and organizing youth events in her local church of KCCC, Aurora. CO.

She continues to climb the ladder of success in Information Technology (Cyber + Security) and follows her quest to write inspiring books for youth and young adults.

www.ingramcontent.com/pod-product-compliance
Lightning Source LLC
Chambersburg PA
CBHW042218050426
42453CB00001BA/10